HEROES OF SCOTLAND

Scotland is a beautiful country of heather covered mountains, shiny lakes, tall castles, remote islands, pretty villages and fantastic cities. It has a stormy, rich past which has made the land and its people very special and unique in the world.

In the pages of this book are tales of bravery and betrayal, stories of monsters, amazing places to visit and colourful customs. You can learn all about Scotland, whilst enjoying the fun games, colouring in and activities.

Contents

Written and designed by William Webb
Illustrated by Les Ives
Published by Colour History Ltd © 2007
Print reference number 29658/04/08

Scotland

Scotland is one of the four countries which make up the United Kingdom. It has 787 islands and the highest mountains in the British Isles including Ben Nevis, which is 1,343 metres high.

Edinburgh is the capital and second largest city and one of Europe's largest financial centres. The biggest city is Glasgow. Greater Glasgow contains nearly half of Scotland's population of five million people. The 'Central Belt' is where most towns and cities lie. Glasgow is in the west, whilst the other main cities of Edinburgh, Dundee and Aberdeen are on the east coast. It has been called 'Fortress Scotland' because of the large number of military bases, nuclear submarines and a nuclear weapons testing range.

Early Scotland
Stone Age settlers built round stone houses, because there was a lack of trees. You can see examples of these at Skara Brae on Orkney. When the Romans invaded Britain in AD 43, part of southern Scotland was briefly controlled by Rome. To the north was Caledonia, which gets its name from the Caledonii tribe. They were one of several fierce 'Picts' or 'Painted Ones'. They lived in tall stone towers called 'brochs' or in smaller 'duns'. Gaelic, or Scots people from Ireland settled in Argyll in the 5th century. The Latin word 'Scotia' means 'Gaelic people' from where we get the name 'Scotland'. By the 9th century they had formed the Kingdom of the Picts and Scots. Viking raiders settled in the far north and western isles and Britons arrived from the south.

The Middle Ages
By the time the Normans conquered England in 1066, Scotland was a united kingdom. They built the first castles to keep control of the country and the Scottish Parliament began to meet around this time. The later Middle Ages were dominated by the 'War for Scottish Independence' against the English, when Robert the Bruce and William Wallace became heroes. By the end of the Middle Ages, Scotland was splitting into two areas, the Scots speaking Lowlands and the Gaelic speaking Highlands, with its warring 'clans'. Clans are family groups who control a region and are led by a chief.

The 'Acts of Union'
In 1603 the King of Scotland, James VI, also became King James I of England. In 1707 the Scottish and English Parliaments produced two 'Acts of Union', which created the Kingdom of Great Britain, with only one Parliament in London.

'The Clearances'
Landowners forced or 'cleared' their land of small farmers so that they could rear sheep on it. Many farmers went to North America, South Africa, New Zealand and Australia, taking their Scottish ways with them.

Modern Scotland
After the Industrial Revolution, Scotland became powerful through its ship building, coal mining and steel industries. After World War II these industries reduced in size. Today, Scotland's importance has grown again through its financial and electronics industries. It has the largest oil reserves in the European Union, as well as natural gas in the North Sea. In 1998 the English Parliament granted Scotland the right to have its own Parliament once more.

The Scottish Parliment
The Scottish Parliament was reconvened in 1999 for the first time in almost 300 years. The Parliament now sits in its new home at the foot of Edinburgh's famous Royal Mile, in front of the spectacular Holyrood Park and Salisbury Crags. The complex building, constructed from a mixture of steel, oak, and granite, is one of the most innovative designs in Britain today. It was opened by Her Majesty the Queen in October 2004.

Arrested for Flag-waving!
The royal flag of Scotland, a yellow banner with a red lion, is often seen at sporting events involving a Scottish team. It is the property of the reigning king or queen of Great Britain. Anyone using the flag without royal permission is breaking the law!

Stone Age settlers built round stone houses because of the lack of trees.

Part of southern Scotland was briefly controlled by Rome. To the north was Caledonia, which gets its name from the Caledonii tribe. They were one of several fierce 'Picts' or 'Painted Ones'.

RUN LADS!

The later Middle Ages were dominated by the 'War for Scottish Independence' against the English, when Robert the Bruce and William Wallace became heroes.

By the time the Normans conquered England in 1066, Scotland was a united kingdom.

Acts of Union

The Scottish and English Parliaments produced two 'Acts of Union' which created the Kingdom of Great Britain.

Landowners forced or 'cleared' their land of small farmers so they could rear sheep on it. Many farmers left Scotland for other countries.

Scotland has the largest oil reserves in the European Union, as well as natural gas, in the North Sea. The Scottish Parliament reconvened in 1999.

Scottish Traditions

The Tartan pattern is made with bands of coloured threads woven at right angles to each other. Tartans today represent a clan, but they may not have originally. By the 1500's, Highland dress included a shirt, tight tartan trousers or 'trews' for the winter and high socks. A cloak or 'plaid' was worn over the shoulder and tucked in at the belt and was used as a blanket or winter covering. The **_kilt_** did not appear until the 16th century. The **_tartan_** was banned during the Jacobite rebellion led by Bonnie Prince Charlie. However, when the ban ended the wearing of Highland dress increased in popularity and The Royal Stewart Tartan is the personal tartan of Queen Elizabeth II.

A Burns Night or 'Burns Supper' is a celebration of the life and poetry of Robert Burns. First started by his friends, it is now celebrated worldwide. A typical evening will include the reading of his poetry and the eating of a **_haggis_**, with **_tatties_** or mashed potatoes and mashed **_neeps_** or swede. Plenty of **_whisky_** will be drunk as well!

The Highland Games are held throughout the year in Scotland and other countries to celebrate Scottish culture. Many events are about feats of strength, such as the **_caber toss_**. Competitors have to throw a large pole or 'caber' so that it circles in the air and both ends hit the ground one after the other. The music of the **_bagpipe_** is a famous symbol of the games and of Scotland itself. The games also feature massed bands and solo musicians and dancing. Scottish country dancing is like ballroom dancing or square dancing. Highland dancing includes the 'Sword Dance' and the **_Highland Fling_**.

The Edinburgh Military Tattoo is a show given by military bands, dancers, musicians and display teams. It is one of many festivals and part of the annual 'Edinburgh Festival' in August. It takes place in the grounds of Edinburgh Castle and is watched on television by millions of people worldwide. Military regiments from other countries and even African tribes have performed at the Tattoo. The top event is the massed pipes and drums of the British Army and soldiers from around the world.

Sport in Scotland is dominated by football, golf and rugby union. The world's first official international football match was held in 1872, in Glasgow between Scotland and England. The score was 0-0. The Scottish Cup is the world's oldest national trophy still in existence. Supporters of the Scotland team are nicknamed the 'Tartan Army'. Glasgow clubs Rangers and Celtic are also called 'the Old Firm' and are the best known Scottish teams. Scotland is also known as the 'Home of Golf' and has world famous golf courses at St Andrews, Carnoustie, Muirfield and Royal Troon.

Haggis, eaten at a Burns Night, is made with the following ingredients: a sheep's heart, liver and lungs, minced with onion, oatmeal, suet, spices and salt. The ingredients are mixed with stock and traditionally boiled using the animal's stomach lining.

Porridge or **_Porage_** is a hot breakfast cereal made by boiling oats in water, milk or both and adding salt.

Scotch Whisky is a world famous drink made from barley, or barley and rye, wheat or corn. It is left for at least three years in oak casks to improve its taste. If the label on the bottle does not say 'Scotch whisky' it was not made in Scotland.

Find the words in the text which are in **_bold italics and underlined_** in the grid below:

A	N	B	A	C	K	K	I	L	T	W	I	G
C	B	A	Y	P	O	R	R	I	D	E	N	R
T	A	T	T	I	E	S	J	W	H	I	T	T
I	G	B	U	K	T	A	R	T	L	H	H	N
P	P	Q	E	X	A	M	I	F	O	G	Q	E
O	I	R	Y	R	R	J	D	I	I	W	U	D
R	P	S	C	U	T	N	N	N	L	H	M	I
R	E	C	H	I	A	O	S	R	A	I	H	N
I	E	O	V	L	N	N	S	T	N	S	A	B
D	R	N	H	R	R	X	E	S	D	K	G	I
G	E	G	L	U	N	Y	E	A	R	Y	G	R
E	I	B	E	O	P	O	R	A	G	E	I	D
H	Z	E	N	T	U	R	N	E	E	P	S	E

There are ten little haggises hidden in this picture - see if you can find them?

Haggis Facts

Many tourists to Scotland are fooled into thinking that a haggis is a three legged Highland animal and have even been led on a 'Wild Haggis Hunt'! In the sport of 'Haggis hurling', contestants have to throw a haggis as far as possible.

Golf and Football Banned!

James II tried to ban golf and football. He said it stopped people practising archery, which was useful in times of war. By contrast James VI, a keen golfer, brought golf to Blackheath in London and turned an Edinburgh bow maker into his golf club maker!

Famous Landmarks

Edinburgh Castle is Scotland's most visited landmark. The 'Crown Room' in the castle contains the Scottish crown jewels. The oldest part is the tiny 12th century St. Margaret's Chapel. Outside the chapel stands the huge 15th century cannon 'Mons Meg'. At one o'clock a gun is fired every day, except Sundays. This was used many years ago to help sailing ships in the Firth of Forth tell the time.

Stirling Castle, like Edinburgh Castle, is in a good defensive position on top of an extinct volcano. Famous battles were fought nearby, such as Stirling Bridge and Bannockburn. A catapult called 'Warwolf', the largest 'trebuchet' ever built, was used against the castle by Edward I. When the defenders saw it they wanted to surrender, but Edward refused. Warwolf destroyed the castle's wall with just one missile!

Balmoral Castle in Aberdeenshire was bought by Queen Victoria's husband Prince Albert and is a favourite summer royal home. Victoria called it "my dear paradise in the Highlands". The large grounds contain red deer and a pine forest and visitors can enjoy fishing, shooting, climbing and guided walks.

Eilean Donan is a beautiful castle in Dornie in the western Highlands of Scotland. It was built as a defence against the Vikings. The Royal Navy destroyed it during the Jacobite rebellion, but it was restored in the 1900's.

Loch Ness is the largest freshwater 'loch' or lake in Britain and is said to be the home of 'Nessie', the Loch Ness Monster. St Columba, a 6th century Irish monk may have saved the life of a Pict who was being attacked by the monster. Since then there have been many sightings and photographs, but today most experts believe that the monster is either a myth or a hoax.

The Forth Rail Bridge is a 'cantilever' bridge connecting Edinburgh with Fife. It was opened in 1890 and is 2.5 km in length. Up to 4,600 workers built it, but nearly 100 of them died during the seven years it took to construct. Some of its steel tubes are as wide as the tunnels in the London Underground.

Chatelherault Country Park in south Lanarkshire contains an 18th century hunting lodge. The lodge was part of a palace, which was demolished to make way for a sand quarry. The quarrying caused the land to move. Now inside the lodge coins will roll across the floor and many visitors report feeling ill!

Traquair House is Scotland's oldest continually inhabited house. It was built in 1107 as a royal hunting lodge and was later used as a hiding place for Catholic priests during Protestant persecutions.

Mull is a wildly beautiful place. The many coloured buildings in its largest town, Tobermory, were the location for the BBC children's series 'Balamory'.

Gretna Green is a small village in the south of Scotland. Traditionally people came to marry here, as Scotland had less strict marriage laws than in England. Today it is still a popular wedding venue with 4,000 weddings taking place every year!

Discovery Point on the bank of the River Tay in Dundee is the home of the ship 'Discovery'. At the end of the 19th century she was used to explore Antarctica under the command of the famous explorer Robert Falcon Scott.

The Steamship Sir Walter Scott has been sailing on the sparkling waters of Loch Katrine in the Trossachs, western Scotland, for over a century. Visitors can sail around the lake in the ship during the summer.

NESSIE: FACT OR FICTION?

Sir Peter Scott, a famous nature expert and painter, gave the monster the scientific name 'Nessiteras rhombopteryx'. In Greek it means 'the wonder of Ness with the diamond shaped fin'. An anagram of the name is 'Monster hoax by Sir Peter S'! Perhaps the most famous 'proof' of Nessie's existence is known as the 'Surgeon's Photograph'. This has since been proven to be a fake. It was actually a clay model attached to a toy submarine! **Do you think the monster really exists? Discuss.**

Stirling Castle

The ship 'Discovery'

The Steamship Sir Walter Scott

Eilean Donan

8

Queen Margaret

Margaret was born into the Anglo-Saxon royal family in 1046 in Hungary. Her family had fled from England when the Danes invaded and the Danish King Cnut became King of England. Margaret returned to England at the age of ten.

When the Normans invaded in 1066 Margaret and her family fled back to Europe, but a storm drove their ship to Scotland. They sought the protection of the Scottish King Malcolm III. Malcolm was about forty years of age and did not have a wife. He was spellbound by the English princess and pursued marriage with the twenty year old. Margaret refused his advances, but eventually gave in and they were married. The great church at Dunfermline is built on the site where the wedding took place.

Margaret was a serious, religious woman. She built many churches and preserved the sacred relics of Catholic saints and part of the cross of Jesus. She may have re-built the monastery on the island of Iona, which had been destroyed by the Vikings. The queen provided a free ferry and housing for pilgrims who came to visit the shrine of Saint Andrew.

Margaret paid the ransoms of English hostages held by the Scots and would personally serve orphans and the poor every day before she herself ate. Every night at midnight she attended church services. She helped bring the English language to Scotland and with the aid of an English priest, who came with her, made the church more Anglo-Saxon and less Gaelic.

Malcolm tried to claim the English throne through his marriage to Margaret. He and their eldest son, Edward, were killed in a battle against the English at Alnwick Castle in Northumbria. At the time Margaret was ill and she died in 1093, three days after hearing of their deaths. Although her remaining children had tried to hide their father and brother's death from Margaret, when she did find out she died of sadness and a broken heart. She was 48.

Margaret was made a saint in 1251 by Pope Innocent IV because of her good life and devotion to the Catholic Church.

A Rare Saint!

Of all the Roman Catholic saints, Queen Margaret stands alone as the happy mother of a large family. She brought up six sons and two daughters and died surrounded by her loving children.

MAKE A CELTIC CROSS

The Gaelic people, who brought Christianity from Ireland, were part of the Celtic peoples of Europe. The Celtic cross was an early symbol of Christianity in Scotland. It is sometimes called 'the cross of Iona'. It was carved in stone and often had 'knot-like' designs on it like the one above. **Copy the shape onto paper, or card and draw your own pattern on the cross.** Some crosses had scenes from Bible stories, which you could put on your cross.

William Wallace

Sir William Wallace led a rebellion against the English occupation of Scotland during the Wars of Scottish Independence. Unlike Robert the Bruce, he was not from the upper classes, but a commoner, or possibly a lower class of noble.

When Wallace was born in 1270 Scotland was ruled by Alexander III. When the king died the next in line to rule was his four year old granddaughter. She died four years later. The Scottish nobles argued about who should become king. They asked King Edward I of England to help settle the argument, but he tried to take control of Scotland instead. He stole the Scottish coronation stone, the 'Stone of Scone' and took it to London. He defeated the Scots in battle and made them promise to be loyal to him.

It is not clear why Wallace started a revolt, but he may have killed some English knights in a quarrel, or perhaps he killed the English governor of Dundee, who had been bullying his family. He and his small band of men defeated the English in several small fights. They cut the English Sheriff of Lanark to pieces in revenge for the murder of Wallace's new wife. They freed many Scottish towns, but a lot of Scottish nobles made peace with the English.

In 1297 Wallace met an English army at the Battle of Stirling Bridge. A Scottish knight on the English side warned the English that it would be dangerous to cross such a narrow bridge to meet the Scottish army. The English ignored his advice and the army crossed the bridge, whilst the Scots held back. When half of the English army had passed, the Scots attacked. They charged at the English and forced them to retreat back on to their own reinforcements who were crossing the bridge. The bridge collapsed under the weight, but it is possible that the Scots may have sabotaged it. The English knights were cut off from help and were speared to death in the river. Their heavy armour made it hard for them to escape and they were easy targets for the lightly armed Scots.

The Hammer

Edward I had these words carved on his gravestone, 'Here is Edward I, Hammer of the Scots'. This was because he managed to keep Scotland under English control, but he never conquered it.

After the battle, Wallace was knighted, possibly by Robert the Bruce. He was named 'Guardian of Scotland and Leader of its Armies'. A year later he lost to the English at the Battle of Falkirk.

In 1305 he was betrayed and captured by a Scottish knight who turned him over to Edward I. He was executed in London and his head was put on a spike on London Bridge. His body was cut up and displayed in the north and in Scotland as a warning to other Scottish rebels.

Where's Wallace?

The English knight on the left is looking for Wallace. Can you guide him through the maze to the Scottish hero in the middle?

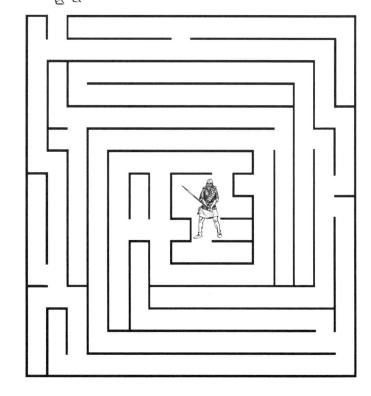

Robert the Bruce

Robert I, also known as Robert the Bruce, was born in 1274. He was the great-great-great-great grandson of King David I of Scotland. His successful wars against the English have made him Scotland's greatest hero.

Although Robert swore he would be loyal to King Edward I of England, in 1297 he joined a rebellion against the English led by William Wallace. So, Edward invaded Scotland. Bruce and many Scottish nobles agreed to be loyal to him in 1302. The next year Edward attacked again. All the Scottish nobles surrendered except William Wallace, but he was captured and executed. Bruce then crowned himself King of Scotland in 1306, at Scone near Perth.

However, he was defeated by the English at the Battle of Methven. The ladies in his family were taken prisoner and he had to hide on the islands west of Scotland. His chance to regain power came when Edward I died leaving his weak son Edward II in charge. During the next three years Bruce captured one English held castle after another, fighting with guerrilla tactics. This meant he did not fight the English on a big battlefield, but his most famous victory was yet to come.

In 1314 Edward sent an army to save the English being besieged at Stirling Castle by Bruce's brother, Edward. Bruce's army was camped near Bannockburn. A young English knight saw the Scottish king inspecting his men and charged at him with his lance. Bruce, armed only with an axe, moved aside, stood up on his stirrups and hit the knight on the helmet, splitting his head in two! This encouraged the Scottish army, who were mainly foot soldiers carrying very long spears. They surged forward and forced the bigger and better armed English army to retreat. The next day the poorly led English failed to beat the fierce Scots. They fled with Edward's bodyguard cutting a path through for their king to escape.

In 1328 the new English king Edward III made peace with Bruce, who was now also King of Ireland. A year later Bruce died leaving his infant son David II to succeed him.

Don't Give Up!

A legend says that after his defeat at the Battle of Methven Bruce hid himself in a cave near Gretna, which you can still visit today. Whilst there, Bruce saw a spider trying to spin a web. Each time the spider failed, it simply started all over again. Inspired by this, Bruce returned to defeat the English armies, which won him more supporters and eventual victory. The moral of this story is, 'if at first you don't succeed, try and try again'.

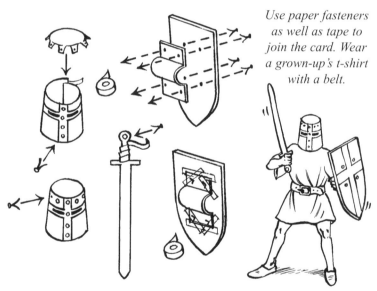

Use paper fasteners as well as tape to join the card. Wear a grown-up's t-shirt with a belt.

MAKE A SUIT OF ARMOUR

Using thin card create a knight's helmet as shown above. With thicker corrugated card build a shield and sword. Decorate the shield with a heraldic design such as a cross, lion, rose, tower or bird. **Then attack your enemy!**

SIR ROBERT DE BRVS!

Robert the Bruce was actually a Norman nobleman called Robert de Brus. He had lands in Scotland, England and France and he spoke French. Queen Elizabeth II is a descendant of Bruce.

Mary, Queen of Scots

Mary I or Mary Stuart, known as the Queen of Scots, was born in 1542. She was the daughter of James V of Scotland and one of Henry VII's great granddaughters. She is one of Scotland's best known monarchs, because her life was full of intrigue.

Mary was only nine months old when her father died, so she was crowned Queen of Scotland in the Chapel Royal at Stirling Castle in 1543. As the Queen was a baby her coronation was the talk of Europe. She was engaged to the heir to the French throne when she was only five years old!

Mary was sent to France where she was well educated and married the future King of France, Francis II. However, when he died in 1561 the French Queen Mother shut Mary out of court life, so Mary returned to rule Scotland. She was tall, elegant and beautiful, in contrast to the rough and tough Scottish nobles who greeted her arrival. Although she began her rule well, things began to go wrong. She married the vain and cruel Lord Darnley who was a Catholic like herself and this upset many of the Protestant nobles.

Mary was very close to an Italian musician, David Rizzio. The nobles thought he was a secret agent for the Pope. They persuaded Darnley to arrange for his murder by telling him that Mary was in love with Rizzio. Rizzio was stabbed to death in front of Mary at a party. Later Darnley was strangled to death and it could have been the Earl of Bothwell who did this. Bothwell married Mary, but this was the final straw for the Scottish nobles. They forced Mary to stop being queen and put her in prison in a castle on an island in the middle of Loch Leven.

She managed to escape disguised as a maid and made her way to England. However, Queen Elizabeth I was suspicious of Mary and had her imprisoned in various castles for the rest of her life. Elizabeth thought Mary might want to take control of Protestant England and turn it into a Catholic country. A serious plot was uncovered to seize the English throne with help from Catholic Spain. Mary was found guilty of treason and was beheaded at Fotheringay Castle in 1587 at the age of 44.

DECIPHER THE CODE

The Catholic assassin Babington sent coded letters to Mary in prison hidden inside a beer keg. Queen Elizabeth's spies discovered the letters and cracked the code. The letter above is similar to one Babington sent to Mary. **Using the key below, find out what the message says. Create your own code and secret messages.**

a = 𝑛   e = 𝜙   i = ✚   o = 𝑓   u = ▢
b = ✚   f = 𝐶   l = ▽   r = 𝖻   w = ✝
c = 𝑂   g = ✝   m = 4   s = 3   x = 𝑛
d = 𝖽   h = ✝   n = 𝜀   t = 𝜎   y = // z = 𝄞

A Messy Execution!

Mary's execution was badly carried out. It took three blows to cut off her head. After the first two blows, Mary was still alive and conscious. The third blow finally took off her head, apart from some gristle, which was cut using the axe as a saw!

Bonnie Prince Charlie

Charles Edward Stuart, known as 'Bonnie Prince Charlie', was born in Rome, Italy, in 1720. At the age of fourteen he took part in his first battle and in 1745 he sailed to Scotland to re-claim the throne for his exiled father, James Stuart.

Catholic Charles had hoped to be supported by a French fleet, but this was badly damaged by storms, so he was left to raise an army in Scotland. This 'Jacobite' rebellion was supported by many Catholic and Protestant Highland clans. Charles captured Edinburgh and defeated the only English army in Scotland at the Battle of Prestonpans. He marched south as far as Derby, but his council advised him to return to Scotland due to the lack of support from English Jacobites.

By now the English king's son, the Duke of Cumberland was chasing Charles and their two armies met at Culloden Moor near Inverness in 1746. The half-starved, outnumbered and unhappy Jacobite army, armed mainly with swords and shields, was slaughtered by the heavy musket and cannon fire of the English. Although he was known by his men as 'Sweet William', the Duke's treatment of the surviving Jacobites was so cruel that he was nicknamed 'Butcher Cumberland'.

After the Battle of Culloden, Bonnie Prince Charlie had to run and hide. Many people such as Flora MacDonald secretly helped him. She took Charles to the Isle of Skye in a small boat disguised as her Irish maid 'Betty Burke'. He eventually escaped to France and spent most of the remainder of his life in exile. Flora was arrested, but she was treated kindly and eventually she was released. Flora was cheered when she entered Edinburgh.

Whilst in exile, Charles turned to heavy drinking. The Pope refused to accept him as heir to the throne of England, Ireland and Scotland, even though he had accepted his father James as the heir. Charles died a sad and lonely man in Rome in 1788.

Just call me 'Charlie'!

If you had to write a letter to Charles you would need a large envelope just to fit his name on it. His full name was Charles, Edward, Louis, John, Casimir, Silvester, Maria Stuart. From his birth he had the titles of 'Prince of England, Scotland, France and Ireland, Duke of Cornwall and Rothesay, Earl of Carrick, Lord of the Isles and Great Steward of Scotland'. He was also named 'Prince of Wales and Earl of Chester'!

The Jacobites

The Jacobites' name came from the Latin word for James, 'Jacobus'. The mainly Catholic Jacobites objected to the replacement of the Stuart King James II of England (James VII of Scotland), with his Protestant daughter Mary II and Mary's husband William of Orange in 1688. The Stuarts lived in exile in Europe after that, trying to regain the throne with the aid of Catholic France or Spain. The emblem of the Jacobites is the White Rose of York and White Rose day is celebrated on 10th June. There are still Jacobite heirs living today, but no one has claimed their right to the English or Scottish throne since the defeat of Bonnie Prince Charlie.

Charlie's Hide-out!

The Isle of Skye is possibly the most romantic of Scottish islands. Dunvegan Castle in the north may be the oldest inhabited castle in Britain. Since 1995 Skye has been linked to mainland Scotland by a bridge, so it is technically not an island now.

Robert Burns

Robert Burns, also known as Rabbie Burns and 'Scotland's favourite son', was born in Alloway in South Ayrshire in 1759. He was the son of a poor farmer who taught Robert and his brother Gilbert. He was to become Scotland's best poet and songwriter.

His family had a hard life as they moved from farm to farm. Burns went to Irvine in the north of the county to become a flax-dresser, a person who prepares flax for spinning into cloth. Unfortunately during New Year celebrations he and his fellow workmen accidentally burned down the business! He began writing poetry, whilst he and his brother struggled to survive after their father's death.

He joined a Freemason's Lodge, which was a secret society for men. He grew in popularity and his poems were well received. Burns became a very important member of the Lodge and read his poems on tours of different lodges all over Scotland. His poems were soon published and he eventually achieved fame as the national poet of Scotland.

In 1786 he went to Edinburgh where he met James Johnson, a struggling music engraver and music seller. They shared a love for old Scottish songs and Burns often wrote lyrics for traditional folk tunes, writing many for The Scots Musical Museum.

He returned to Ayrshire and married Jean Armour and the couple went to live on a farm near Dumfries. He later gave up the farm and became a taxman. Towards the end of his life Burns lost some friends because of some of his opinions and his support of the French Revolution. His health worsened and he became quite depressed and took to heavy drinking. He died in 1796. Within a short time of his death, money started pouring in from all over Scotland to support his widow and children.

His memory is celebrated by Burns clubs across the world. His birthday is an unofficial national day for Scottish people and those with Scottish ancestry enjoy 'Burns suppers'. His poem and song, 'Auld Lang Syne' is often sung at 'Hogmanay', the Scottish New Year celebration.

A WEE BEASTIE!

Burns wrote many of his poems in Scots. He wrote about a mouse he scared whilst ploughing and described it as a 'Wee, sleekit, cow'rin, tim'rous Beastie', which in English is a 'tiny timorous forlorn beast'. Match the **Scots** words on the left to the **English** words on the right:

auld	waulie	*thirsty*	*whom*
drouthy	twa	*long*	*devil*
back-yett	sark	*rags*	*jolly*
rair	crooning	*drop*	*humming*
deil	creechie	*well*	*greasy*
naig	drap	*shirt*	*old*
wham	duddies	*gate at the back*	

Scotland's Second Best Poet

William Topaz McGonagall (1830 - 1902) was a Scottish weaver, actor and poet. He is renowned around the world as one of the worst poets in the English language, but he is actually Scotland's best selling poet after Burns! He had no sense of humour and no talent, but despite this he continually asked Queen Victoria if he could be her official poet!

He believed in his talent even when his audience were pelting him with eggs and vegetables. He also had an unusual acting career. He had to pay the theatre to play the part of Macbeth in Shakespeare's famous play. In one performance, even though Macbeth is supposed to be murdered, McGonagall refused to die!

Harry Potter!

J.K. Rowling, the author of the Harry Potter books, chose the surname of the Professor of Transfiguration, Minerva McGonagall, because she had heard of McGonagall and loved the surname.

Greyfriars Bobby

In 1858 John Grey, an Edinburgh policeman, died and was buried in Greyfriars churchyard in the Old Town of Edinburgh. Few people attended the funeral and his grave was a simple one. His Skye terrier dog, called Bobby spent the rest of his life sitting on his master's grave, sleeping there at night and only leaving for his food. He would stay whatever the weather, although he may have spent very cold winters in nearby houses. Dogs were not allowed in the graveyard, so the caretaker tried at first to get rid of Bobby.

However, the caretaker was touched by the dog's devotion to his master and eventually he let him stay. When it was pointed out that an ownerless dog should be put down, the Lord Provost of Edinburgh, Sir William Chambers paid for Bobby's licence. After fourteen years of faithfully attending his master's grave, Bobby died. He was buried near his master and on his gravestone it says, 'Let his loyalty and devotion be a lesson to us all'. A statue and fountain were built in his memory and can still be seen today.